THE LOVE PARADOX

EXPLORING THE GAP BETWEEN EXPECTATIONS AND REALITY IN RELATIONSHIPS

PROF S. N. SINGH

Made with ♥ on the Notion Press Platform
www.notionpress.com

Contents

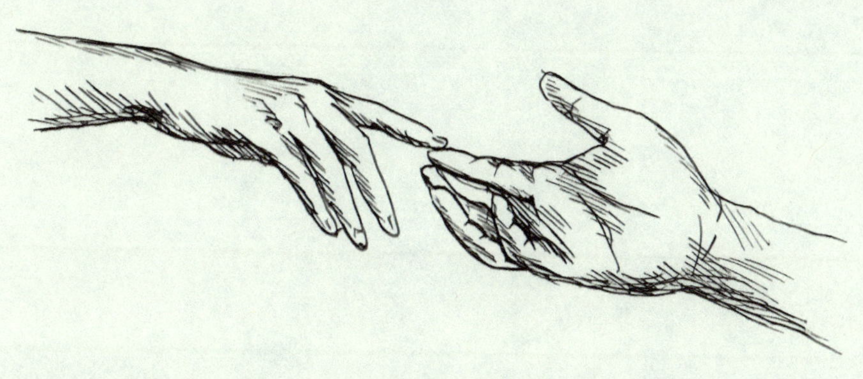

"Love is not just a feeling, it's a choice to navigate the gap between expectations and reality"

- Prof S.N. Singh

Preface

"The Love Paradox: Exploring the Gap between Expectations and Reality in Relationships" is a book that explores the complexities and challenges of modern relationships. In today's world, relationships have become increasingly complex, with high expectations and societal pressures affecting the way we view and experience love. This book delves into the reasons why relationships often fail and provides readers with a deeper understanding of the love paradox and the various factors that contribute to it.

Throughout this book, readers will learn about the unrealistic expectations and societal norms that often lead to disappointment and frustration in relationships. They will also be given practical tools and insights to help them navigate the gap between expectations and reality and build stronger, more fulfilling relationships. Whether you're looking for a deeper understanding of love and relationships, or simply seeking practical tips for improving your own relationships, this book is an essential guide for anyone seeking to deepen their connection with themselves and others.

So, whether you're single or in a relationship, this book is a must-read for anyone looking to create meaningful and lasting connections in their life. Join us on this journey of self-discovery as we explore the love paradox and the many challenges and opportunities that come with it

Introduction – Defining The Love Paradox And The Challenges Of Modern Relationships

Love is one of the most fundamental and universal human experiences. It has the power to bring us incredible joy, happiness, and fulfillment, and it is an essential part of what makes us human. At the same time, however, love can also be one of the most complicated and challenging aspects of our lives. Relationships can be filled with misunderstandings, disagreements, and disappointment, and it can often be difficult to find a path to lasting love and happiness.

In the modern world, this challenge is compounded by a number of factors, including the influence of technology and social media, societal pressure, and the impact of past experiences and cultural norms. As a result, it is becoming increasingly difficult for people to navigate the complexities of modern love and find the connection and happiness they seek. This disconnect between our expectations and reality is what we refer to as the love paradox.

The love paradox is a challenge that affects us all, regardless of our age, gender, or sexual orientation. It is a reminder that the journey to love and happiness is not always a smooth one, and that there are many obstacles and pitfalls that we must navigate along the way. But, despite these challenges, there is still hope.

In this book, we will explore the love paradox and the challenges of modern relationships in depth, and provide readers with practical strategies and tools for bridging the gap between expectations and reality. We will start by examining the root causes of relationship problems, including unrealistic expectations, societal pressure, and the impact of past experiences, and provide readers with a deeper understanding of why relationships can be so difficult.

Next, we will delve into the importance of effective communication and emotional intelligence in relationships. We will explore the role of active listening, empathy, and mindfulness in building stronger connections and improving understanding between partners. We will also provide readers with practical exercises and techniques for developing their emotional intelligence and learning to manage their own emotions in a healthy and effective manner.

Finally, we will explore the path to lasting love and happiness, and provide readers with practical tips and strategies for building strong, fulfilling relationships based on mutual understanding, trust, and acceptance. Whether you're single, in a relationship, or somewhere in between, this book will provide you with the guidance you need to navigate the complexities of modern love and find the connection and happiness you seek.

So, let's embark on a journey together to explore the love paradox and discover a path to lasting love and happiness. With the right tools and understanding, you can overcome the challenges of modern relationships and build the life-long connection you desire.

"The beauty of relationships lies in the vulnerability and courage it takes to love, the growth it brings, and the happiness it creates. Embrace the journey and never give up on love..."

CHAPTER II

The Roots of the Love Paradox: Understanding the Causes of Relationship Problems

Unrealistic Expectations

Expectations play a critical role in our relationships, shaping the way we perceive and respond to our partners and the world around us. Unfortunately, many of us hold unrealistic expectations about love, relationships, and the people we choose to spend our lives with. These unrealistic expectations can lead to disappointment, frustration, and a feeling of disconnection from our partners and the world around us.

In this chapter, we will examine the impact of unrealistic expectations on our relationships and explore the ways in which these expectations can contribute to the love paradox. We will start by looking at the role of cultural norms and societal expectations in shaping our perceptions of love and relationships. For example, we will discuss how media depictions of love and relationships, such as Hollywood romance movies and fairy tales, can create unrealistic expectations that can be difficult to live up to in real life.

Next, we will delve into the impact of personal experiences and past relationships on our expectations in love. We will explore how our childhood experiences, past relationships, and other formative experiences can shape our beliefs and expectations about love, and how these expectations can affect our current relationships. We will also discuss the role of personal insecurities, such as fear of rejection or abandonment, in creating unrealistic expectations about love and relationships.

Finally, we will examine the ways in which unrealistic expectations can lead to disappointment and frustration in our relationships. We will discuss the impact of unrealistic expectations on communication, trust, and intimacy, and explore how these unrealistic expectations can create a feeling of disconnection and isolation from our partners. We will also provide readers with practical strategies for identifying and managing unrealistic expectations in their relationships.

In conclusion, unrealistic expectations play a critical role in shaping our relationships and can contribute to the love paradox. By understanding the impact of cultural norms, past experiences, and personal insecurities on our expectations, we can develop a deeper understanding of the ways in which unrealistic expectations can affect our relationships and take steps to manage these expectations in a healthy and effective manner. This is an important first step towards bridging the gap between expectations and reality in our relationships and finding lasting love and happiness.

The impact of technology and social media on relationships

In today's world, technology and social media play a significant role in our daily lives, and this is especially true when it comes to our relationships. From online dating to virtual communication, technology has changed the way we interact with others and form connections. While these advancements have brought many benefits, they have also introduced new challenges and complexities into our relationships.

One of the key ways that technology and social media impact relationships is through their ability to create unrealistic expectations. Social media, in particular, is often seen as a highlight reel of our lives, showcasing the best moments, achievements, and relationships of others. This can lead us to compare our own lives and relationships to the lives and relationships of others, which can be damaging to our self-esteem and our relationships. Furthermore, online dating has created a culture of instant gratification, where we can swipe through countless profiles and options, searching for the perfect partner. This endless search for the perfect match can lead to a never-ending cycle of disappointment and dissatisfaction in our relationships.

Another impact of technology and social media on relationships is the way it has changed the way we communicate. In the past, we communicated primarily in person or through written correspondence, which allowed for a greater level of nuance, empathy, and understanding in our conversations. With technology, however, our communication has become more impersonal and less meaningful, with emojis and short texts replacing face-to-face conversations and handwritten letters. This shift in communication can lead to misunderstandings, miscommunications, and a lack of deeper connection in our relationships.

Social media have become a ubiquitous presence in our lives, influencing how we interact with each other and shaping our relationships in countless ways. While these platforms can provide many benefits, such as allowing us to connect with friends and family who live far away or fostering a sense of community and support, they can also have a significant impact on our romantic relationships.

One of the most notable effects of technology and social media on relationships is the way they affect our communication patterns. With so many distractions and the ease of communication through texting, social media, and other forms of online messaging, it can be difficult to have meaningful, face-to-face conversations with our partners. This can lead to a breakdown in communication, as well as misunderstandings and miscommunications.

Another impact of technology and social media is the way they can create unrealistic expectations and comparisons with others. Social media platforms are often curated to showcase the highlights of people's lives, leading us to believe that everyone else is living a happier, more fulfilling life than we are. This can result in feelings of inadequacy, insecurity, and dissatisfaction in our relationships.

Additionally, technology and social media can also contribute to infidelity in relationships. With so many ways to connect with others online, it can be easy to develop emotional or physical relationships with people outside of our primary relationships. This can result in trust issues, broken hearts, and the end of relationships.

Despite the challenges that technology and social media present, they can also be used in positive ways to strengthen our relationships. For example, couples can use social media to stay connected when they're apart, or they can use it to share experiences and memories with each other. Technology can also provide opportunities for couples to have virtual date nights, or to try out new activities and hobbies together, even if they're not physically together.

Additionally, technology and social media can also lead to the creation of virtual relationships that are not rooted in reality. For example, people may form close relationships with others through online communities or social media, only to find that these relationships lack depth and substance when they meet in person. These virtual relationships can also distract us from the real-life relationships that matter most to us, leading us to neglect the people and connections that truly matter in our lives.

So what can we do to mitigate the negative impact of technology and social media on our relationships? One solution is to limit our exposure to social media and technology, setting boundaries around when and how we use these tools in our relationships. Another solution is to cultivate real-life relationships, putting effort into face-to-face communication and making time for the people who matter most to us. Finally, we can also work to shift our perspective, focusing on what is real and meaningful in our relationships, rather than what is portrayed on our screens.

In conclusion, technology and social media have had a profound impact on our relationships, both positive and negative. By being aware of these impacts and taking steps to mitigate the negative effects, we can build stronger, more fulfilling relationships in the modern world.

Societal pressure and cultural norms

Society and culture play a significant role in shaping our perceptions of love and relationships. Cultural norms and societal expectations can create unrealistic ideals about what a relationship should look like and the roles that each partner should play. These unrealistic expectations can put pressure on individuals in relationships to conform to societal norms, leading to disappointment and frustration when reality does not match expectations.

In this chapter, we will explore the impact of societal pressure and cultural norms on relationships. We will start by examining the role of media in shaping our perceptions of love and relationships. For example, we will discuss how Hollywood romance movies and fairy tales often depict love as a perfect, fairy-tale romance, creating unrealistic expectations that can be difficult to live up to in real life.

Next, we will delve into the impact of cultural expectations on relationships. We will examine how cultural norms around gender roles, expectations for marriage and family life, and attitudes towards sexuality and intimacy can shape our perceptions of relationships. We will also explore the impact of societal expectations for success and achievement on relationships, and how these expectations can create additional pressure and stress for individuals in relationships.

Finally, we will examine the ways in which societal pressure and cultural norms can lead to disappointment and frustration in relationships. We will discuss the impact of unrealistic expectations on communication, trust, and intimacy, and explore how societal pressure and cultural norms can create a feeling of disconnection and isolation from our partners. We will also provide readers with practical strategies for managing the impact of societal pressure and cultural norms in their relationships.

In conclusion, societal pressure and cultural norms play a significant role in shaping our perceptions of love and relationships. By understanding the impact of these societal pressures and cultural norms, we can develop a deeper understanding of the ways in which they can affect our relationships and take steps to manage them in a healthy and effective manner. This is an important first step towards bridging the gap between expectations and reality in our relationships and finding lasting love and happiness.

Past experiences and emotional baggage

One of the biggest challenges in modern relationships is the impact of past experiences and emotional baggage on our current relationships. Our past experiences, whether they be positive or negative, shape the way we view and interact with the world around us, and this is especially true when it comes to our relationships. For example, if we've had a series of negative past relationships, we may come into new relationships with a fear of being hurt again, which can lead us to shut down emotionally or become overly guarded. On the other hand, if we've had a series of positive past relationships, we may have high expectations for what love and relationships should be like, which can lead to disappointment and frustration when those expectations are not met.

In order to fully understand the impact of past experiences and emotional baggage on our relationships, it's important to take a closer look at what these terms mean. "Past experiences" refer to the experiences, events, and relationships that have shaped us in the past, while "emotional baggage" refers to the psychological and emotional scars that we carry with us as a result of these experiences. This emotional baggage can include things like fear, anger, sadness, and guilt, and it can have a significant impact on our ability to form healthy, happy relationships in the present.

To effectively navigate the gap between expectations and reality in relationships, it's important to recognize and address the emotional baggage that we carry with us. This may involve engaging in therapy, self-reflection, or other forms of personal growth and self-discovery. It may also involve actively working to let go of past hurts and traumas, and learning to trust and open ourselves up to new experiences. Ultimately, the goal is to develop a healthier relationship with ourselves and with others, and to build stronger, more fulfilling relationships in the present and future.

CHAPTER III

Questions to Ask Yourself

1: In your relationships, which is more often the case: your expectations are met, or they are not met?

A. Expectations are mostly met

B. Expectations are mostly not met

C. Expectations are sometimes met, sometimes not met

2: When it comes to emotional baggage in relationships, which statement do you agree with most?

A. I don't have any emotional baggage from past experiences.

B. I have some emotional baggage, but it doesn't impact my current relationships.

C. I have significant emotional baggage from past experiences that affects my current relationships.

3: In resolving conflicts in relationships, how often do you rely on mindfulness techniques?

A. Rarely

B. Sometimes

C. Always

4: How often do you practice self-reflection in your relationships?

A. Rarely

B. Sometimes

C. Often

5: How has technology and social media impacted your relationships?

A. It has had a positive impact.

B. It has had a neutral impact.

C. It has had a negative impact.

6. What is your biggest challenge in relationships?

a) Communication

b) Trust

c) Setting boundaries

d) Balancing individuality and intimacy

7. How often do you reflect on your past experiences and emotions in relationships?

a) Rarely

b) Sometimes

c) Often

d) Regularly

8. On a scale of 1-5, how comfortable are you with expressing vulnerability in relationships?

a) 1 (Not comfortable at all)

b) 2

c) 3

d) 4

e) 5 (Very comfortable)

9. What role do you believe technology and social media play in relationships?

a) Positive

b) Neutral

c) Negative

10. How important is mindfulness in resolving conflicts and building stronger connections in your relationships?

a) Not important

b) Somewhat important

c) Very important

d) Essential

11. How do you currently handle expectations and realities in your relationships?

12. How do societal pressures and cultural norms impact your relationships?

____

____

____

____

____

13. To what extent do past experiences and emotional baggage influence your current relationships?

____

____

____

____

____

14. How has technology and social media affected your relationships and communication with others?

____

____

____

____

____

15. How comfortable are you with vulnerability and opening up in your relationships?

16. How do you approach resolving conflicts in your relationships?

17. How mindful are you in your relationships and daily life?

18. How do you prioritize self-reflection and personal growth in your relationships?

19. How do you celebrate diversity and inclusion in your relationships?

____

____

____

____

____

20. What are your thoughts on Professor S.N. Singh's approach to relationships and what can you take away from this book to apply to your own life?

____

____

____

____

____

CHAPTER IV

The Art of Communication: Improving Understanding and Connecting with Your Partner

The importance of active listening

One of the most important components of any relationship, whether romantic or otherwise, is effective communication. However, in order to have effective communication, it is crucial to be an active listener. Active listening involves not only hearing what someone is saying, but also actively engaging with and trying to understand their perspective.

One of the benefits of active listening is that it helps to build trust and respect between partners. When one person feels heard and understood, they are more likely to feel valued and appreciated. This, in turn, creates a sense of emotional safety and security, which can foster a deeper and more meaningful connection.

Another benefit of active listening is that it can help to resolve conflicts and misunderstandings. When both partners are actively listening to each other, they are more likely to understand each other's perspectives and find common ground. This can lead to more productive and respectful conversations, and can help to prevent conflicts from escalating.

However, active listening is not always easy. In the heat of an argument or disagreement, it can be tempting to jump to conclusions, interrupt each other, or dismiss each other's perspectives. It takes practice and effort to really listen to what someone is saying, and to put your own thoughts and emotions aside in order to fully understand their point of view.

To practice active listening, try to put your phone away, turn off the TV, and give your full attention to the person speaking. Encourage them to express themselves fully, and try not to interrupt or dismiss their thoughts. Repeat back what you've heard to show that you understand, and ask clarifying questions if you need to. Additionally, try to put yourself in their shoes and imagine what it would be like to have their experiences and feelings.

In conclusion, active listening is a critical component of any relationship, as it helps to build trust and respect, resolve conflicts, and foster deeper connections. By making an effort to listen actively and truly understand each other's perspectives, we can create and maintain strong, healthy relationships.

"Love is not about finding someone who completes you, it's about finding someone who accepts you for who you are and inspires you to become the best version of yourself..."

The role of empathy in relationships

Empathy is a critical component of healthy relationships. It involves the ability to understand and share in the feelings and experiences of others, and it is essential in building strong and meaningful connections with our partners. When we practice empathy in our relationships, we show that we care about our partner's feelings and experiences, and we create a space where they feel safe and understood.

One of the ways in which empathy can improve relationships is by reducing conflict. When we take the time to understand our partner's point of view, we are less likely to react impulsively and more likely to find common ground and work towards a resolution that benefits both parties. This can help to reduce the frequency and intensity of arguments and disagreements, leading to a more harmonious relationship.

Another important benefit of empathy in relationships is that it promotes deeper levels of intimacy and connection. When we listen to our partners, show them that we care about their feelings and experiences, and make an effort to understand where they are coming from, we create a deeper level of trust and emotional intimacy. This can lead to a stronger, more meaningful bond between partners.

Empathy also helps to foster a sense of empathy and compassion in relationships. When we practice empathy, we become more aware of the feelings and experiences of others, and we are more likely to respond to their needs in a supportive and understanding way. This can help to create a supportive and nurturing environment in relationships, which is essential for building a healthy and sustainable partnership.

While empathy is a critical component of healthy relationships, it is also important to remember that it is a skill that can be learned and developed over time. By making a conscious effort to practice empathy in our relationships, we can work to create more meaningful and fulfilling connections with our partners. Whether it is through active listening, trying to understand our partner's point of view, or simply making an effort to show that we care about their feelings, there are many ways to cultivate empathy in our relationships.

In conclusion, the role of empathy in relationships is vital to building strong and meaningful connections with our partners. By being empathetic, we can reduce conflict, foster deeper levels of intimacy and connection, and create a supportive and nurturing environment in our relationships. With practice, empathy can become an integral part of our relationships, helping us to create and maintain healthy, fulfilling partnerships for years to come.

Techniques for effective communication

Effective communication is a key factor in any successful relationship, whether it's a romantic partnership, a friendship, or a familial bond. The way we communicate with each other can have a profound impact on our relationships, influencing the way we feel about ourselves, each other, and the world around us.

One technique for effective communication is active listening. This means truly paying attention to what the other person is saying, without interrupting or formulating a response in your head before they've finished speaking. When we actively listen, we show the other person that we value and respect their perspective, and we create an environment where both partners feel heard and understood.

Another technique for effective communication is being clear and specific about what we want to communicate. This means avoiding vague statements or accusations, and instead being straightforward about what we're feeling, what we need, or what we're hoping for. By being specific and clear in our communication, we can avoid misunderstandings and help the other person to better understand what we're trying to convey.

It's also important to communicate openly and honestly in relationships. This means avoiding the use of passive-aggressive behavior or manipulation, and instead being upfront and direct about our feelings and needs. Open and honest communication can help to build trust, create a sense of intimacy, and prevent misunderstandings and conflicts from arising.

Another important technique for effective communication is taking responsibility for our own emotions. This means recognizing that our feelings are our own, and not the result of someone else's actions or words. By taking responsibility for our emotions, we can avoid blaming others and instead focus on finding ways to resolve conflicts and improve the relationship.

Finally, it's important to seek to understand the other person's perspective, even if we don't agree with it. This can be done by asking questions, paraphrasing what the other person has said, or simply trying to see things from their point of view. When we make an effort to understand the other person's perspective, we can create an environment of mutual respect, which can help to build stronger, healthier relationships.

In conclusion, effective communication is a critical component of any successful relationship. By utilizing techniques such as active listening, clear and specific communication, open and honest dialogue, taking responsibility for our own emotions, and seeking to understand the other person's perspective, we can work to create and maintain strong, healthy relationships with the people in our lives.

"Love is the greatest adventure of all, full of twists and turns, but always leading us to a place of growth, happiness, and fulfillment. So let's embrace it with open hearts and a spirit of joy, and create our own love story to remember..."

Navigating difficult conversations

Difficult conversations are an inevitable part of any relationship, but they can often be difficult to navigate, leading to misunderstandings, hurt feelings, and even the end of a relationship. Whether it's discussing a sensitive topic, expressing disappointment, or addressing a relationship issue, having these conversations can be challenging, but they are necessary for maintaining a healthy and fulfilling relationship.

One of the biggest challenges in having difficult conversations is finding the right time and place to talk. It is important to choose a time when both partners are calm, relaxed, and not under stress, as this will make it easier to have a productive and meaningful conversation. Additionally, choosing a private, quiet place where you won't be interrupted is also important, as this will help to create an environment that is conducive to open and honest communication.

Another challenge in having difficult conversations is finding the right words to use. It is important to approach the conversation with empathy, understanding, and respect, rather than with anger, blame, or defensiveness. Using "I" statements, such as "I feel hurt when..." or "I would like to discuss...", can be a helpful

way to express yourself, as it focuses on your feelings and needs, rather than blaming your partner.

When having difficult conversations, it's also important to listen actively. This means putting aside your own thoughts and feelings, and focusing on what your partner is saying. By actively listening, you can gain a deeper understanding of their perspective, and this can help to find common ground and come to a resolution.

Finally, it's important to be willing to compromise and find solutions that work for both partners. Relationships are about give and take, and being open to finding a solution that works for both partners can help to resolve the issue and strengthen the relationship. It's also important to be patient, as difficult conversations often take time, and it may take several attempts to find a resolution that works for both partners.

In conclusion, while difficult conversations can be challenging, they are an important part of any relationship, and navigating them effectively can help to maintain a strong and healthy relationship. By approaching these conversations with empathy, respect, and a willingness to compromise, partners can work together to find solutions and build a more fulfilling relationship.

CHAPTER V

Emotional Intelligence: Understanding and Managing Your Own Emotions

The definition of emotional intelligence

Emotional intelligence is a concept that has gained a lot of attention in recent years, with many people recognizing its importance in personal and professional success. But what exactly is emotional intelligence?

Emotional intelligence can be defined as the ability to recognize, understand, and manage our own emotions, as well as the emotions of others. This involves being able to identify and label our emotions, understand why we feel the way we do, and use this knowledge to guide our thoughts, behaviors, and actions.

Emotional intelligence also involves the ability to understand and respond appropriately to the emotional expressions of others. This requires being able to accurately interpret nonverbal cues and body language, as well as being able to effectively communicate our own emotions and respond to the emotional needs of others.

There are several components that make up emotional intelligence, including self-awareness, self-regulation, motivation, empathy, and social skills. Self-awareness refers to the ability to understand our own emotional states and how they impact us and those around us. Self-regulation involves the ability to control our emotional responses, rather than letting our emotions control us. Motivation refers to the drive to pursue our goals, even in the face of emotional challenges. Empathy involves the ability to understand and respond to the emotional needs of others, while social skills involve the ability to build and maintain strong, healthy relationships.

Having emotional intelligence is important for many reasons. It can help us to better understand ourselves and others, leading to stronger and more fulfilling relationships. It can also help us to effectively manage our own emotions, reducing the impact of stress and anxiety on our lives.

Additionally, having high emotional intelligence is often associated with greater success in both personal and professional contexts.

In conclusion, emotional intelligence is a complex and multifaceted concept that involves the ability to recognize, understand, and manage our own emotions, as well as the emotions of others. By developing our emotional intelligence, we can work to improve our relationships, manage our emotional responses more effectively, and achieve greater success in all areas of our lives.

The benefits of emotional intelligence in relationships

Emotional intelligence (EI) refers to the ability to recognize and understand one's own emotions, as well as the emotions of others. In the context of relationships, EI can be a powerful tool for creating and maintaining healthy, fulfilling connections with our partners.

One of the key benefits of EI in relationships is improved communication. When we are able to understand and empathize with our partner's feelings, it becomes easier to have meaningful and productive conversations. This can help to resolve conflicts more effectively and prevent misunderstandings from escalating.

Another benefit of EI in relationships is increased intimacy and emotional connection. When we are attuned to our own emotions and those of our partners, we are able to build a deeper sense of trust and intimacy. This allows us to feel more connected to our partners and to experience a greater sense of emotional fulfillment in the relationship.

EI can also play a role in preventing relationship problems from arising in the first place. By being self-aware and attuned to the emotional needs of our partners, we are better equipped to navigate challenging situations and maintain a strong, healthy connection. This can help to keep the relationship on track and prevent it from becoming derailed by unnecessary conflicts or misunderstandings.

Finally, EI can also help to promote resilience in relationships. When we are able to understand and manage our own emotions, we are less likely to become overwhelmed by stress or negativity. This, in turn, helps us to remain stable and focused, even in the face of challenges.

In conclusion, emotional intelligence is a crucial component of healthy, fulfilling relationships. By developing our EI skills, we can create stronger connections with our partners, improve communication, and promote greater emotional resilience. These benefits can help us to maintain strong, healthy relationships, even in the face of adversity.

Techniques for developing emotional intelligence

Emotional intelligence is the ability to identify, understand, and manage our own emotions and the emotions of others. It is a key factor in building healthy relationships and is essential for personal growth and fulfillment. Unfortunately, many of us struggle to develop our emotional intelligence and may feel overwhelmed by our emotions, leading to stress, anxiety, and relationship difficulties.

However, with practice and dedication, it is possible to develop our emotional intelligence and strengthen our relationships. Here are some techniques that can help:

Mindfulness: Mindfulness is the practice of bringing our attention to the present moment and observing our thoughts and feelings without judgment. By becoming more mindful of our emotions, we can gain greater control over them, reducing our stress levels and improving our relationships.

Emotional vocabulary: One way to develop emotional intelligence is to expand our emotional vocabulary. This means learning to recognize, label, and describe our emotions and those of others, which can help us understand them better and respond in a more thoughtful and effective way.

Empathy: Empathy is the ability to understand and share the feelings of others. To develop empathy, it can be helpful to try to put ourselves in others' shoes, to listen actively, and to communicate in a way that demonstrates that we understand and care about the other person's feelings.

Self-reflection: Self-reflection is the process of taking time to think about our thoughts, feelings, and behaviors and how they relate to our relationships and experiences. By reflecting on our emotions, we can gain insight into why we react the way we do, and learn how to manage our emotions in a more productive and healthy way.

Practice active listening: Active listening involves giving our full attention to the person speaking and engaging in the conversation in a way that shows we are truly listening and interested. By practicing active listening, we can develop our emotional intelligence by becoming better at understanding the emotions of others and learning how to respond in a supportive and empathetic way.

These are just a few of the techniques that can help us develop our emotional intelligence. By incorporating these practices into our daily lives, we can become more self-aware, reduce our stress levels, and strengthen our relationships.

Coping with negative emotions in relationships

Negative emotions are a normal part of any relationship, but they can also be challenging to manage. Whether it's anger, frustration, sadness, or disappointment, dealing with these emotions in a healthy and productive way can be the key to maintaining a strong and lasting relationship.

One effective way to cope with negative emotions in relationships is to communicate openly and honestly with your partner. This means expressing your feelings in a non-blaming way and giving your partner the opportunity to do the same. When both partners feel heard and understood, it can be easier to find solutions to problems and to reduce the impact of negative emotions.

Another important tool for coping with negative emotions is self-reflection. Taking time to reflect on your own thoughts and feelings can help you to better understand why you're feeling a certain way and what you need to do to feel better. This may include practicing self-care, such as exercise, meditation, or therapy, or it may mean working to identify and challenge negative thought patterns that may be contributing to your feelings.

In addition to communicating and self-reflection, it can also be helpful to seek support from outside sources. This can include talking to friends or family members, or working with a therapist or counselor. These outside perspectives can provide valuable insights and guidance, as well as a safe and supportive space to process and work through negative emotions.

Ultimately, the key to coping with negative emotions in relationships is to approach them with empathy and compassion, both for yourself and for your partner. By working together to understand and manage your emotions, you can build a stronger and more resilient relationship that can weather any storm.

In conclusion, negative emotions are a normal part of any relationship, but they don't have to have a negative impact. By communicating openly, practicing self-reflection, and seeking support, couples can effectively manage negative emotions and create a strong and healthy relationship that can endure for years to come.

CHAPTER VI

Mindfulness: A Path to Acceptance and Understanding

The definition of mindfulness and its benefits

Mindfulness is a concept that has gained a lot of attention in recent years, and for good reason. At its core, mindfulness is the practice of being present and fully engaged in the moment, without judgment or distraction. It is a way of paying attention to our thoughts, emotions, and experiences, without getting caught up in them or allowing them to control us.

When it comes to relationships, mindfulness can have a profound impact. By being mindful in our interactions with our partners, we are able to be more fully present, to listen more deeply, and to respond in ways that are grounded in love and compassion. We are also better able to manage our emotions and to avoid getting caught up in negative thought patterns or cycles of conflict.

The benefits of mindfulness in relationships are numerous. For one, it can help us to build greater intimacy and connection with our partners, as we are more able to be fully present and to understand their perspective. It can also help to reduce stress and conflict, as we are better able to manage our emotions and to respond in ways that are grounded in love and compassion.

Mindfulness can also help us to cultivate a sense of inner peace and well-being, which can spill over into our relationships. When we are mindful, we are less likely to be reactive, and more likely to respond in ways that are grounded in love and compassion. This can help to create a sense of safety and security in our relationships, which is essential for long-term happiness and well-being.

Overall, mindfulness is a powerful tool for enhancing our relationships, by helping us to be more fully present, to manage our emotions, and to cultivate greater intimacy and connection. By incorporating mindfulness into our relationships, we can build strong, loving, and fulfilling relationships that last a lifetime.

The role of mindfulness in relationships

Mindfulness has become increasingly popular in recent years as a way to improve overall health and well-being. However, its benefits extend far beyond just the individual, and it can also play a crucial role in strengthening relationships.

When we practice mindfulness, we become more aware of our thoughts, feelings, and behaviors, and can more effectively manage them in the moment. This awareness can help us to avoid reactive, knee-jerk responses to conflicts or challenges in our relationships, and instead approach them with a clear and calm mind.

In addition, mindfulness can help us to develop greater empathy and understanding towards our partners. When we are present in the moment and paying attention to our own and our partner's emotions and experiences, we are better equipped to communicate effectively and resolve conflicts in a healthy and positive way.

Furthermore, mindfulness can help to reduce stress and increase emotional regulation, leading to greater relationship satisfaction and happiness. When we are calm and centered, we are more able to respond to challenges in our relationships in a positive and effective way, rather than allowing stress and negative emotions to take control.

Another important aspect of mindfulness in relationships is the ability to cultivate gratitude and appreciation for our partners. When we are mindful, we are able to see the beauty and value in each moment, including the moments we spend with our partners. This helps to foster a sense of love and appreciation, which is essential for maintaining a strong and loving relationship.

Finally, mindfulness can help us to cultivate greater self-awareness and personal growth, leading to more fulfilling relationships. When we are mindful, we are able to understand and regulate our emotions and behaviors, which in turn can lead to greater self-confidence and improved communication skills, essential components of healthy relationships.

In conclusion, mindfulness has the potential to play a transformative role in relationships. By fostering greater awareness, empathy, and regulation, it can lead to stronger, more fulfilling relationships that are built on love, trust, and mutual understanding.

Practical exercises for developing mindfulness in relationships

One of the key components of healthy relationships is mindfulness, or the ability to be present and aware in the moment. Mindfulness can help us to navigate the gap between our expectations and the reality of our relationships, as well as to embrace vulnerability and open up to love. In this chapter, we will explore practical exercises that can help us to develop mindfulness in our relationships.

Meditation and Mindfulness Practices: Meditation and mindfulness practices can help us to become more present and aware in our relationships. This can include regular meditation sessions, mindfulness exercises such as deep breathing, and practicing mindfulness in our daily activities such as eating, walking, or doing household chores. By becoming more mindful in our daily lives, we can cultivate a greater sense of presence and awareness in our relationships.

Communication Skills: Effective communication is a key aspect of mindfulness in relationships. This includes active listening, expressing our needs and feelings in a clear and non-threatening manner, and avoiding communication patterns that can lead to conflict and distance. Practicing active listening, assertiveness, and other communication skills can help us to maintain a mindful and connected relationship with our partner.

Boundary Setting: Mindfulness in relationships also involves setting healthy boundaries and respecting our partner's boundaries. This can include defining physical, emotional, and spiritual boundaries, and being willing to negotiate and modify them as needed. By setting and respecting healthy boundaries, we can cultivate a relationship that is based on mutual respect and trust.

Emotional Intelligence: Emotional intelligence refers to the ability to recognize and understand our own emotions, as well as the emotions of others. Practicing emotional intelligence in our relationships can help us to navigate conflicts and build greater intimacy and connection. This can involve learning to identify and regulate our emotions, as well as empathy and compassion for our partners.

Gratitude Practices: Practicing gratitude can help us to cultivate a more positive and mindful outlook in our relationships. This can include daily gratitude journaling, expressing gratitude to our partners, and focusing on the positive aspects of our relationships. By cultivating gratitude, we can shift our focus from the challenges of our relationships to the gifts and blessings that they bring.

By incorporating these practical exercises into our relationships, we can cultivate greater mindfulness and connection, and navigate the gap between our expectations and the reality of our relationships. These exercises can help us to embrace vulnerability, open up to love, and build stronger, more fulfilling relationships.

The importance of mindfulness in resolving conflict and building stronger connections

Conflict is an inevitable part of any relationship, and it is important to have the tools and skills to effectively handle and resolve it. One key tool in conflict resolution is mindfulness. Mindfulness is the practice of being present in the moment and paying attention to our thoughts, emotions, and sensations without judgment.

In relationships, mindfulness can help us to become more aware of our own thoughts, feelings, and behaviors, as well as those of our partners. This awareness allows us to respond more effectively to conflicts and to build stronger connections with our partners.

One of the key benefits of mindfulness in relationships is improved communication. By being present and aware, we are able to listen to our partners with empathy and understanding, rather than being defensive or reactive. This improved communication can help to reduce misunderstandings and conflicts, and to build stronger connections.

Mindfulness can also help us to manage our emotions in conflict situations. When we are mindful, we are less likely to react impulsively and instead are able to respond with thoughtfulness and consideration. This can help us to resolve conflicts in a more constructive and collaborative manner, and to avoid causing harm to our relationships.

In addition to resolving conflict, mindfulness can also help us to strengthen the emotional bond between partners. When we are mindful, we are more attuned to our partners' needs and feelings, and we are better able to show empathy and support. This increased emotional connection can deepen our relationships and help us to build a strong foundation of trust and love.

Another benefit of mindfulness in relationships is improved self-awareness. When we practice mindfulness, we become more aware of our own thoughts, feelings, and behaviors, and how they impact our relationships. This self-awareness can help us to make positive changes in our relationships, such as becoming more patient, understanding, and loving towards our partners.

In conclusion, mindfulness is a powerful tool for resolving conflict and building stronger connections in relationships. By being present and aware, we are able to communicate more effectively, manage our emotions, deepen our emotional connections, and improve our self-awareness. Practicing mindfulness can help us to create healthier and more fulfilling relationships, and to experience the love and connection that we all seek.

27

Building Strong, Fulfilling Relationships: Strategies for Navigating the Love Paradox

Accepting and embracing reality

One of the biggest challenges in relationships is the tendency to hold onto unrealistic expectations and hopes, rather than accepting the reality of our situation. This can lead to disappointment, frustration, and a feeling of unfulfillment in our relationships. However, by embracing reality and learning to accept the truth about our relationships, we can create stronger and more satisfying connections with our partners.

One of the first steps to accepting reality in relationships is to examine our own beliefs and expectations. We often carry preconceived notions about what a relationship should be, based on cultural norms, societal expectations, and our own past experiences. These expectations can create an unrealistic standard that is difficult to live up to, and can lead to disappointment and frustration.

In order to accept reality, it is important to understand that relationships are complex and dynamic, and that no two relationships are exactly alike. Rather than focusing on what we think our relationship should be like, we need to focus on what it is, and work together to build the best relationship possible.

Another important aspect of accepting reality is to acknowledge and embrace our partner's flaws and imperfections. No one is perfect, and trying to change or hide our partner's imperfections can only lead to disappointment and frustration. By embracing and accepting each other's differences, we can create a foundation of trust and respect that is essential for a healthy relationship.

In addition to accepting reality in our relationships, it is also important to embrace the present moment and avoid living in the past or worrying about the future. This can be a challenge, especially in a world that is constantly changing and evolving. However, by living in the present and focusing on what is happening now, we can create a deeper connection with our partners and enjoy the moment.

Finally, accepting and embracing reality in relationships also involves accepting the impermanence of all things. Relationships can change and evolve over time, and it is important to be open to these changes and not cling too tightly to the past. By being open to the changes that come with time, we can create a relationship that is adaptable and resilient, and that will stand the test of time.

In conclusion, accepting and embracing reality is an essential aspect of healthy relationships. By examining our beliefs and expectations, embracing our partner's flaws and imperfections, living in the present moment, and being open to change, we can create a foundation of trust, respect, and love that will sustain us for a lifetime.

The importance of mutual understanding and respect

In any relationship, mutual understanding and respect are essential components of a healthy and happy partnership. Without these two elements, relationships can quickly become strained, leading to conflict, resentment, and ultimately, the breakdown of the relationship.

One of the primary ways in which mutual understanding and respect are expressed in relationships is through active and engaged communication. When partners listen to each other, truly hear what each other is saying, and respond in a thoughtful and respectful manner, they create a foundation for mutual understanding. This understanding helps partners to better understand each other's perspectives, beliefs, and needs, leading to a deeper sense of empathy and compassion for one another.

Another aspect of mutual understanding and respect is the way that partners support each other in pursuing their individual goals and aspirations. Whether it's supporting each other in their careers, encouraging each other in personal pursuits, or simply being there to lend a listening ear, showing support and respect for each other's dreams and aspirations is a crucial part of any strong relationship.

In addition to fostering mutual understanding and respect, it is also important for partners to make an effort to understand each other's individual experiences and perspectives. This means being open to learning about each other's backgrounds, cultures, and life experiences, and making an effort to understand how these experiences have shaped each partner's perspective. By doing this, partners can gain a deeper appreciation for each other and avoid making assumptions or judgments based on stereotypes or misconceptions.

Another aspect of mutual understanding and respect is being able to resolve conflicts in a healthy and productive manner. When partners approach conflicts with a focus on understanding each other's perspectives and finding mutually beneficial solutions, they are able to work through disagreements and challenges without damaging their relationship.

"Love is the most powerful force in the world, capable of healing even the deepest wounds and transforming the most broken of hearts. Embrace it, nurture it, and let it guide you to the happiness you deserve."

Finally, mutual understanding and respect also involves being there for each other through the ups and downs of life. Whether it's through offering comfort and support during difficult times, or celebrating each other's successes, partners who show mutual understanding and respect are able to build a strong, supportive, and resilient relationship.

In conclusion, mutual understanding and respect are critical components of any healthy and happy relationship. By fostering open and engaged communication, supporting each other in individual pursuits, understanding each other's experiences and perspectives, resolving conflicts in a healthy manner, and being there for each other through the ups and downs of life, partners can create a foundation for a strong and fulfilling relationship.

Finding balance and building trust

One of the biggest challenges in any relationship is finding balance. With busy schedules, demanding careers, and an abundance of distractions, it can be difficult to find the time and energy to prioritize our relationships. At the same time, trust is an essential component of any healthy relationship, and building trust takes time, effort, and dedication.

Finding balance in a relationship requires a combination of self-awareness, open communication, and mutual respect. It's important for each partner to understand their own needs and boundaries, and to communicate those to the other person. Additionally, couples should make time for each other, both for romantic and non-romantic activities, in order to build and maintain their connection.

When it comes to building trust, honesty is key. It's important for both partners to be transparent about their thoughts, feelings, and actions, and to make a conscious effort to be reliable and trustworthy. Building trust also involves being able to handle conflicts and disagreements in a healthy and productive way, without letting those conflicts turn into arguments or causing harm to the relationship.

Another aspect of building trust is being able to share intimate details and personal information with each other. This level of vulnerability can be difficult, but it is essential for creating a deep, meaningful connection with your partner. Sharing personal experiences and emotions with each other can help build trust, as well as deepen the emotional bond between partners.

In addition to honesty and open communication, physical intimacy can also play a key role in building trust. Touch is a powerful form of nonverbal communication, and physical affection can help strengthen the bond between partners and build trust in the relationship. However, it's important for both partners to be comfortable with the level of physical intimacy in the relationship, and to communicate their boundaries and needs.

Finally, trust in a relationship can also be strengthened by understanding and accepting each other's flaws and limitations. No one is perfect, and it's important to acknowledge and accept each other's imperfections, rather than trying to change each other. By accepting each other for who you are, you can build a deeper, more meaningful connection and increase trust in the relationship.

In conclusion, finding balance and building trust in relationships takes time, effort, and commitment. However, by prioritizing your relationship, communicating openly and honestly, and being supportive and understanding of each other, you can build a strong, healthy relationship based on trust and mutual respect.

"Love is not just a feeling, it's a choice we make every day to put in the effort, to be vulnerable, to grow, and to never give up on the ones we care about. Make that choice, and watch your relationships blossom into something beautiful..."

Embracing vulnerability and opening up to love

One of the biggest challenges in relationships is allowing ourselves to be vulnerable and open to love. We all carry emotional baggage from past experiences, whether it's from past relationships, childhood traumas, or other life events. This baggage can prevent us from opening up and being fully invested in our relationships, leading to a lack of intimacy and a feeling of emotional distance from our partners.

However, in order to build strong, healthy relationships, it is essential to embrace vulnerability and let go of our emotional baggage. This means being willing to share our deepest thoughts and feelings with our partners, even when it is scary or uncomfortable. By doing so, we open up the possibility for true intimacy and connection, which is the foundation of a strong and loving relationship.

Embracing vulnerability also means being willing to face our fears and insecurities, and to work through them in our relationships. This can include confronting past traumas, learning to trust our partners, and being willing to be vulnerable and honest about our emotions. By doing so, we open ourselves up to experiencing true love and connection, rather than being trapped in a cycle of fear and distance.

Another aspect of embracing vulnerability is the willingness to forgive and let go of past hurt. Holding onto grudges and resentments can prevent us from moving forward and being open to new relationships. Forgiveness can be difficult, but it is a crucial step in the process of embracing vulnerability and opening up to love. By letting go of past hurt, we create space in our hearts and minds to experience the joy and happiness of new relationships.

One of the most effective ways to embrace vulnerability and build healthy relationships is through therapy or counseling. Talking with a trusted therapist or counselor can help you work through past traumas and insecurities, and to develop the skills and confidence needed to be vulnerable and open in your relationships. Whether you are in a relationship or single, therapy can be an excellent way to develop self-awareness and build healthy, loving relationships.

Another way to embrace vulnerability is through mindfulness and self-reflection. Taking time to reflect on your emotions and thoughts can help you to better understand your own vulnerabilities and insecurities, and to work through them in a healthy and productive way. Practicing mindfulness can also help you to cultivate compassion and understanding for yourself and others, which is crucial in building strong and loving relationships.

Finally, embracing vulnerability also means being open to learning and growing in your relationships. This can include seeking out workshops, books, and other resources to help you deepen your understanding of relationships, as well as being willing to take an active role in your own growth and development. By continually working on yourself and your relationships, you can create a foundation of love and connection that will last a lifetime.

In conclusion, embracing vulnerability and opening up to love is a crucial step in building strong and healthy relationships. Whether you are single or in a relationship, this process requires courage, self-awareness, and a willingness to face your fears and insecurities. But by doing so, you can experience true intimacy, connection, and love in your life.

CHAPTER VIII

Overcoming Insecurities and Building Trust

Trust is the foundation of any healthy and fulfilling relationship. Without trust, there can be no emotional intimacy, mutual respect or true connection. Insecurity, on the other hand, can erode trust and create distance and distrust. In this chapter, we will explore how to overcome insecurities and build trust in relationships.

First, it is important to understand the root causes of insecurity. Insecurity can stem from a variety of sources, including past experiences, childhood trauma, cultural influences, and self-esteem issues. It is essential to identify and address these underlying causes in order to overcome insecurities.

One effective way to build trust is through open and honest communication. Sharing your feelings, thoughts, and experiences with your partner can help to increase mutual understanding and emotional intimacy. However, it is also important to listen actively and be empathetic to your partner's perspective.

Another way to build trust is through consistent and reliable behavior. This includes following through on commitments and promises, being dependable, and consistently demonstrating your love and support for your partner. It is also important to demonstrate authenticity and vulnerability, allowing your partner to see the real you and build a deeper connection.

Forgiveness is another critical component of building trust. Holding onto grudges, resentments, and negative feelings can erode trust and create distance in a relationship. Instead, it is essential to practice forgiveness, letting go of the past and focusing on the present moment.

Finally, building trust takes time and effort, and it is important to be patient and understanding. Trust can be broken and repaired, but it takes time and consistent effort to rebuild.

In conclusion, overcoming insecurities and building trust are critical components of any healthy and fulfilling relationship. By identifying the root causes of insecurity, practicing open and honest communication, being dependable, forgiving, and being patient, couples can work together to build a strong foundation of trust and emotional intimacy.

CHAPTER IX

Finding Balance in Life and Love

Finding balance in life and love is a complex and ongoing process that requires effort and dedication from both partners. In many cases, individuals are faced with competing demands on their time and energy, including work, relationships, hobbies, and personal responsibilities. Striving to maintain balance between these competing demands can be a constant challenge, and it's easy to feel overwhelmed and stressed.

For relationships, finding balance is crucial for creating a strong, healthy bond between partners. When one partner feels like they are giving more than they are receiving, resentment can begin to build. On the other hand, when both partners feel like they are contributing equally, it can help create a sense of stability and support in the relationship.

One of the key components of finding balance in life and love is establishing clear priorities and setting boundaries. This involves making decisions about what is most important to each individual, and working together to make sure that these priorities are aligned. For example, if one partner places a high value on their career, while the other values spending time with family, it is important to find a way to accommodate both of these needs. This may involve creating a schedule that allows for flexible work hours, or making an effort to carve out time for family activities.

Another important aspect of finding balance in life and love is maintaining a healthy work-life balance. For many individuals, work can consume a significant amount of time and energy, leaving little room for other important aspects of life. To counteract this, it's important to set aside dedicated time for relationships, hobbies, and self-care. This can involve creating a routine or schedule that prioritizes these activities, or finding ways to incorporate them into daily life.

For relationships, finding balance also involves striking a balance between alone time and together time. Spending time apart allows partners to recharge and pursue their own interests, while spending time together can help build and strengthen the bond between partners. Additionally, finding a balance between giving and receiving in a relationship is critical. This involves creating a dynamic where both partners feel like they are contributing and receiving support, without one partner feeling like they are doing all the heavy lifting.

CHAPTER X

Mindful Intimacy: Connecting with Our Partners on a Deeper Level

Intimacy is an essential component of any relationship. It encompasses emotional, physical, and spiritual connections that bring people closer together and strengthen the bond between them. But, in a world that prioritizes external validation and fast-paced lifestyles, cultivating intimacy can often be challenging. This is where mindfulness comes in.

Mindfulness is a practice of focusing on the present moment and being fully aware of one's thoughts, feelings, and experiences. When applied to relationships, it can help individuals to deepen their connections with their partners, build trust and emotional intimacy, and improve their overall satisfaction in the relationship.

In this chapter, we will explore the concept of mindful intimacy and how it can enhance relationships. We will discuss various mindfulness exercises and practices that individuals can adopt to deepen their connections with their partners. These practices include:

Mindful listening: Encouraging partners to listen to each other without judgment, distraction or interruption.

Shared mindfulness practices: Engaging in mindfulness exercises together, such as meditation, yoga or deep breathing.

Sensory exploration: Encouraging partners to explore and connect with their senses, such as touch, taste, and scent.

Gratitude practice: Expressing gratitude for each other and for the relationship regularly.

Mindful communication: Encouraging partners to communicate openly, honestly and non-judgmentally.

By incorporating these practices into daily life, individuals can cultivate a deeper sense of intimacy and connection with their partners. Additionally, they can develop more compassion and empathy for each other, leading to a more harmonious and fulfilling relationship.

Moreover, mindfulness also helps individuals to become more aware of their own thoughts and emotions, reducing the chances of misunderstandings and conflicts. This can lead to a more peaceful and stress-free relationship.

Additionally, mindful intimacy can also improve the physical aspects of relationships, such as sexual intimacy. When individuals are more mindful of their own bodies and sensations, they are more likely to experience pleasure and intimacy on a deeper level.

In conclusion, incorporating mindfulness into relationships can have a profound impact on the quality of the relationship. By fostering deeper connections and understanding between partners, mindful intimacy can help individuals to build strong and fulfilling relationships that last a lifetime.

It is essential to note that mindful intimacy is not a one-time solution, but rather a continuous practice that requires effort and commitment from both partners. However, by making a conscious effort to prioritize intimacy and connection, individuals can reap the benefits of a stronger and more fulfilling relationship.

CHAPTER XI

The Art of Compromise and Negotiation

In relationships, the art of compromise and negotiation is crucial for the growth and longevity of the relationship. It is essential for individuals to understand that in any relationship, both partners have unique wants, needs, and opinions, and it is essential to find a way to reconcile these differences. In this chapter, we will delve into the art of compromise and negotiation and the role it plays in building and maintaining healthy relationships.

The Importance of Compromise:

Compromise is essential in any relationship because it allows both partners to feel heard and respected. When we compromise, we are demonstrating that we are willing to give up something of our own for the benefit of the relationship. It is crucial to understand that compromise is not a sign of weakness but rather a sign of strength and maturity. When both partners are willing to compromise, it leads to a deeper understanding and stronger bond between them.

The Art of Negotiation:

Negotiation is a vital aspect of compromise. It is a means of finding a solution that works for both partners. Negotiating involves listening to each other's needs, wants, and concerns and finding a way to reconcile these differences. In a relationship, both partners should be able to negotiate with each other in a calm, respectful, and non-confrontational manner. Negotiation helps individuals understand each other's perspectives and find a common ground.

The Role of Communication:

Effective communication is essential in compromise and negotiation. It is imperative to communicate openly, honestly, and respectfully to achieve a resolution that works for both partners. Communication should be used to express one's needs, wants, and concerns and to listen to the needs and wants of the other partner. Good communication leads to a deeper understanding of each other's perspectives and allows for an amicable resolution.

Benefits of Compromise and Negotiation:

Compromise and negotiation bring several benefits to a relationship. It strengthens the bond between partners, improves communication, increases trust, and helps build a healthier relationship. By learning to compromise and negotiate, individuals can resolve conflicts and build stronger connections.

Conclusion:

In conclusion, the art of compromise and negotiation is crucial for the growth and longevity of any relationship. By compromising and negotiating, individuals can resolve conflicts and build stronger connections. It is essential to understand that compromise and negotiation are not signs of weakness but rather signs of strength and maturity. By embracing the art of compromise and negotiation, individuals can build healthier, happier, and more fulfilling relationships.

CHAPTER XII

The Role of Forgiveness and Letting Go

Forgiveness and letting go are two important aspects of a healthy relationship. In many cases, holding on to past hurts, grudges, and resentment can have a negative impact on the current relationship and prevent partners from moving forward. In this chapter, we will explore the role of forgiveness and letting go in resolving conflict, improving communication, and fostering a deeper sense of intimacy between partners.

First, it's important to understand what forgiveness is and what it isn't. Forgiveness is not about condoning or forgetting past wrongs, but it's about letting go of anger and resentment towards the person who caused the hurt. By doing this, we are able to free ourselves from the negative emotions that have been holding us back and create a space for more positive feelings, such as compassion and empathy.

Forgiveness is also a two-way street. Both partners must be willing to let go of past hurts and work towards resolving the conflict. This means being open and honest about one's feelings and needs, and being willing to listen to the other person's perspective.

One way to practice forgiveness is through mindfulness. By being present in the moment and focusing on our thoughts and emotions, we can gain a greater understanding of what is causing us to feel hurt or resentful. This can also help us to identify any patterns or behaviors that need to be addressed in order to move forward.

Another important aspect of forgiveness is letting go. This means releasing the hold that past hurts and grudges have on our lives and our relationships. Letting go can be a difficult process, but it is necessary in order to create a more positive and loving environment between partners. This can involve having honest conversations with each other, seeking outside support, or engaging in therapy to work through the feelings and emotions that are holding us back.

In conclusion, forgiveness and letting go are essential components of a healthy and loving relationship. By practicing these skills, we can work towards resolving conflicts, improving communication, and fostering a deeper sense of intimacy between partners. Through mindfulness and openness, we can free ourselves from past hurts and embrace a brighter future together.

CHAPTER XIII

Navigating Life Transitions and Maintaining Connection

Life is full of changes, and relationships can be affected in many ways by these changes. Whether it's a new job, a move, a new baby, or a major health crisis, transitions can put stress on even the strongest relationships. But with the right tools and techniques, couples can successfully navigate these changes and maintain a strong connection.

The first step in navigating life transitions is to recognize and acknowledge that change is inevitable. It's important to approach these changes with an open mind and a willingness to adapt. This can mean learning new skills, rethinking old habits, or finding new ways to communicate and connect.

One of the keys to maintaining a strong connection during life transitions is effective communication. Couples should make time to talk about their feelings, fears, and concerns, and be open and honest about what they need from each other. This can help to avoid misunderstandings and conflict, and can strengthen the bond between partners.

It's also important to make time for each other during life transitions. Whether it's taking a walk together, having a date night, or simply cuddling on the couch, taking time to focus on each other can help to keep the connection strong.

Another key to successfully navigating life transitions is to seek support from others. This can mean talking to friends, family, or a therapist, or joining a support group. Having a supportive network can help couples to stay strong and feel less isolated during challenging times.

In addition to seeking support, it's important to take care of oneself during life transitions. This can mean making time for exercise, relaxation, or other self-care activities. It's also important to stay connected with one's own values and priorities, and to maintain a positive outlook and a sense of humor.

Finally, it's important to celebrate the positive aspects of life transitions, and to look for opportunities for growth and learning. This can mean finding new ways to connect with one's partner, exploring new interests and hobbies, or taking advantage of new experiences and opportunities.

Navigating life transitions can be challenging, but with the right tools and techniques, couples can maintain a strong connection and grow even closer as they navigate these changes together. By focusing on effective communication, seeking support, taking care of oneself, and celebrating the positive aspects of change, couples can successfully navigate life transitions and build a lasting, fulfilling relationship.

CHAPTER XIV

Finding Balance in Life and Love

"Balance is not something you find, it's something you create"

Life is a journey, and relationships are an integral part of it. However, it is not uncommon for individuals to struggle in finding the right balance between their personal and professional lives, and their relationships. Balancing work, family, friends, hobbies, and intimate partnerships can be a challenge, but it is essential for a healthy and fulfilling life.

In this chapter, we will explore the importance of finding balance in life and love and how it can positively impact our relationships. We will discuss the common struggles people face in maintaining this balance and provide practical tips for overcoming these challenges.

The first step in finding balance is to understand your priorities and values. You need to be clear about what is important to you, and what you want to achieve in life. This will help you make informed decisions and prioritize your time effectively.

Next, it is essential to learn to say no. With so many demands on our time and attention, it is easy to become overwhelmed. By learning to say no to the things that do not align with our values and goals, we can create more time and energy for the things that matter most to us.

It is also crucial to set realistic goals and expectations for ourselves and those around us. By establishing clear and achievable goals, we can reduce the stress and pressure we put on ourselves and our relationships.

It is essential to carve out time for self-care and personal growth. Whether it is exercise, meditation, or a hobby, finding time to focus on our well-being can improve our mood and energy levels, and ultimately enhance our relationships.

Additionally, it is important to maintain open and honest communication with our partners. By discussing our goals and challenges, we can work together to find ways to support each other and achieve a healthy balance in life and love.

Another key factor in finding balance is to manage our stress levels. Stress can have a significant impact on our relationships, so it is essential to find healthy ways to cope with stress and prevent burnout.

Finally, finding balance in life and love is a continuous journey, and it is important to be flexible and adapt to change. By maintaining a positive attitude, being patient, and seeking help when needed, we can find balance and create fulfilling and long-lasting relationships.

In conclusion, finding balance in life and love is essential for a healthy and fulfilling life. By understanding our priorities, learning to say no, setting realistic goals, focusing on self-care, and maintaining open and honest communication, we can create a balance that benefits both ourselves and our relationships.

CHAPTER XV

Celebrating Diversity and Inclusion in Relationships

One of the most important aspects of a healthy and thriving relationship is understanding and embracing diversity and inclusion. The world is full of diverse people with unique backgrounds, cultures, experiences, and perspectives. When two individuals come together in a relationship, it is crucial that they celebrate this diversity and create an inclusive environment where both partners feel comfortable, valued, and understood.

The first step in creating an inclusive relationship is to educate ourselves about different cultures and experiences. This means being open to learning about different beliefs, values, and traditions, and being willing to listen to and understand the perspectives of others. It also means being mindful of our own biases and prejudices and working to overcome them.

Inclusion in a relationship also involves creating a space where both partners feel free to express themselves and be their authentic selves. This means being respectful and non-judgmental when it comes to differences in opinions, beliefs, and lifestyles. It also means being willing to compromise and make accommodations for each other when necessary.

Another important aspect of celebrating diversity and inclusion in relationships is to recognize and respect each other's unique backgrounds, experiences, and identities. This includes acknowledging and valuing each other's different cultural, racial, and religious backgrounds, as well as their unique sexual orientations, gender identities, and abilities.

One of the key benefits of embracing diversity and inclusion in relationships is that it helps to build stronger connections and foster greater understanding between partners. When both partners feel valued, respected, and understood, it creates a deeper sense of trust, intimacy, and emotional connection. This in turn leads to a more fulfilling and satisfying relationship, as both partners are able to be their true selves and feel supported in their individual journeys.

In conclusion, celebrating diversity and inclusion in relationships is crucial for building strong, healthy, and fulfilling relationships. It involves being open to learning about and understanding different perspectives, creating an inclusive environment where both partners feel comfortable, and embracing each other's unique backgrounds, experiences, and identities. By doing so, partners are able to build deeper connections, foster greater understanding, and create a more fulfilling and satisfying relationship.

CHAPTER XVI

The Benefits of Self-Reflection and Personal Growth

Self-reflection and personal growth are critical components of a healthy and fulfilling life, and they play an important role in the success of relationships as well. In this chapter, we will explore the benefits of engaging in self-reflection and personal growth and how they can lead to more meaningful and satisfying relationships.

Self-reflection involves taking a step back and evaluating one's thoughts, emotions, and behaviors in order to gain a deeper understanding of oneself. This process of introspection allows individuals to identify areas where they may need to change or improve in order to live a more fulfilling life. When it comes to relationships, self-reflection can help individuals recognize patterns of behavior that may be negatively impacting their connections with others. For example, someone who struggles with trust issues may find that self-reflection helps them to understand why they have difficulty opening up to others and what they can do to overcome this challenge.

Personal growth, on the other hand, refers to the ongoing process of developing one's skills, knowledge, and abilities in order to achieve their goals and reach their full potential. When it comes to relationships, personal growth can help individuals to better understand their needs and desires, as well as to identify the skills they need to achieve their goals. For example, someone who wants to improve their communication skills may benefit from attending a workshop or taking a course on effective communication.

There are several benefits to engaging in self-reflection and personal growth, including:

Improved self-awareness: By taking the time to reflect on one's thoughts, emotions, and behaviors, individuals can gain a better understanding of who they are and what drives them. This increased self-awareness can help individuals to make more informed decisions and to avoid behaviors that may be harmful to themselves or to others.

Increased self-esteem: Engaging in self-reflection and personal growth can help individuals to feel more confident and capable, leading to increased self-esteem. When individuals feel good about themselves, they are more likely to approach relationships with a positive attitude, which can help to build stronger and more fulfilling connections with others.

Improved relationships: By gaining a better understanding of oneself, individuals are better equipped to understand and connect with others. When individuals are able to identify and work through their own emotional baggage, they are less likely to project their issues onto their partners, which can help to create more harmonious and fulfilling relationships.

Increased emotional intelligence: Self-reflection and personal growth can help individuals to become more in touch with their emotions and to understand the emotions of others. This increased emotional intelligence can lead to better communication, conflict resolution, and overall relationship satisfaction.

Better stress management: When individuals are able to identify their own emotional triggers and work through them, they are better equipped to manage stress and avoid burnout. This, in turn, can help to create a more positive and healthy environment in their relationships.

In conclusion, self-reflection and personal growth are critical components of a healthy and fulfilling life, and they play an important role in the success of relationships. By taking the time to reflect on one's thoughts, emotions, and behaviors, individuals can gain a deeper understanding of themselves, improve their relationships, and achieve greater overall satisfaction and happiness.

CHAPTER XVII

The Future of Relationships in a Rapidly Changing World

"The future of relationships lies in our ability to adapt, evolve, and grow together as individuals and as a society"

In this chapter, we will explore the various ways in which relationships are evolving in our rapidly changing world. With advancements in technology, shifts in societal norms and values, and the increasing pace of life, the nature of relationships is undergoing a radical transformation.

One of the most significant changes is the increasing use of technology in relationships. From dating apps to social media, technology has dramatically altered the way people form and maintain relationships. While technology has certainly made it easier to connect with others, it has also created new challenges. For example, social media can create unrealistic expectations and foster comparisons, while dating apps can contribute to a culture of superficiality and a focus on appearance over genuine connection.

Another important factor shaping the future of relationships is shifting societal norms and values. For example, more and more people are choosing to remain single, choosing careers and personal fulfillment over traditional romantic relationships. Additionally, there is a growing recognition of the importance of diversity, with an increasing acceptance of different relationship models such as polyamory and open relationships.

As our world continues to change, it is crucial that individuals and couples alike stay informed and adapt to the new realities of relationships. In this chapter, we will delve into the ways in which technology, societal norms, and other factors are shaping the future of relationships, and discuss the steps that individuals can take to navigate these changes and build strong, fulfilling relationships in this rapidly evolving world.

Finally, we will consider the ways in which the principles explored in this book - embracing vulnerability, practicing mindfulness, embracing self-reflection and personal growth, and rejecting unrealistic expectations - can help individuals and couples build the relationships of the future. Whether navigating the challenges of technology or embracing new societal norms, the tools and strategies presented in this book will equip readers with the tools and knowledge necessary to build strong, healthy, and meaningful relationships in the 21st century.

CHAPTER XVIII

The Joy of Building a Lasting and Fulfilling Relationship

"Building a lasting and fulfilling relationship requires effort, patience, and above all, the joy of being with someone who brings out the best in you and makes your heart sing with happiness..."

Building a lasting and fulfilling relationship is one of the most rewarding experiences one can have in life. It requires effort, patience, and a deep understanding of oneself and one's partner. However, the rewards are many: companionship, love, support, and the sharing of life's experiences.

At the heart of a lasting and fulfilling relationship is a foundation of trust, communication, and mutual respect. When these elements are in place, partners are able to navigate challenges and conflicts, and work together to build a stronger and more satisfying bond.

One key factor to building a lasting and fulfilling relationship is self-awareness. It is important to understand one's own thoughts, emotions, and behaviors, and how they may impact the relationship. This can include recognizing patterns of behavior that may be harmful or disruptive to the relationship, and taking steps to change them.

Another important element is communication. Good communication skills are vital for navigating challenges and expressing one's needs and desires in a clear and respectful manner. It is important for partners to take the time to listen to each other, and to make an effort to understand their perspectives.

Additionally, partners should work to cultivate mutual respect and trust. Trust is built through consistency, reliability, and honesty, and requires time and effort to develop. In a trusting relationship, partners are able to be vulnerable with each other, and to share their innermost thoughts and feelings. This helps to deepen the connection and creates a sense of intimacy that is essential for a lasting and fulfilling relationship.

It is also important for partners to have a shared vision for their relationship, and to work together to achieve common goals. This can include things like mutual support in pursuing personal interests and careers, creating a stable home environment, and making time for each other. When partners have a sense of shared purpose, they are able to weather challenges and maintain a strong connection even during difficult times.

Finally, it is important to celebrate the joys of the relationship. Whether it is through small acts of kindness, or through special milestones, it is important to take the time to acknowledge and appreciate the happiness that is brought into our lives by our relationships.

In conclusion, building a lasting and fulfilling relationship requires effort, patience, and a commitment to personal growth and self-awareness. When partners are able to bring these qualities to their relationship, they are able to create a bond that is strong, loving, and enduring. The joy of building such a relationship is a reward that cannot be measured, and one that brings happiness and fulfillment to our lives.

CHAPTER XIX

Conclusion: The Future of Relationships and the Love Paradox

"Love is not a destination, but a journey that grows stronger with each step taken in the right direction."

Reflections on the journey to lasting love

The journey towards lasting love is often not a straightforward one. Relationships are complex and filled with ups and downs, and navigating them can be a challenge. However, by reflecting on our experiences and learning from them, we can gain insights into what it takes to build a strong, loving relationship.

One of the key reflections on the journey to lasting love is the importance of self-awareness. By understanding our own emotions, needs, and values, we can better understand what we want from our relationships, and what we need to do to make them successful. This self-awareness also allows us to recognize patterns in our behavior and relationships, and to make changes that can lead to better outcomes.

Another reflection on the journey to lasting love is the importance of communication. Good communication is essential for any relationship, and it is crucial for resolving conflicts and building trust and intimacy. When we are able to openly and honestly communicate with our partners, we can work through challenges and build a stronger, more resilient relationship.

Reflecting on our past experiences can also help us identify areas that need improvement. For example, if we have a tendency to avoid conflict or to struggle with trust, we can work on these areas in order to build a healthier, more loving relationship. This can include seeking therapy or other forms of support, as well as making changes in our own behavior and attitudes.

Finally, reflecting on the journey to lasting love can help us appreciate the importance of self-care. When we take care of ourselves, both physically and emotionally, we are better equipped to handle the challenges of relationships and to build strong, loving connections with others. This includes activities such as exercise, spending time with loved ones, and engaging in self-reflection and mindfulness practices.

In conclusion, reflecting on the journey to lasting love is an ongoing process that requires us to be open, honest, and self-aware. By reflecting on our experiences and learning from them, we can gain the insights and skills we need to build strong, healthy relationships that can stand the test of time.

The role of growth and self-discovery in relationships

One of the key aspects of healthy relationships is growth and self-discovery. As individuals, we are constantly evolving and changing, and it is important that our relationships grow and evolve along with us. This means being open to exploring new ideas and perspectives, as well as being willing to examine our own beliefs and behaviors.

One important aspect of growth and self-discovery in relationships is personal growth. This means taking the time to reflect on our own experiences and emotions, and to understand the impact that our past experiences and relationships have had on us. By doing so, we can learn from our past mistakes and make positive changes in our lives and in our relationships.

Another aspect of growth and self-discovery is exploring new interests and passions. This can include taking up new hobbies, traveling to new places, or learning new skills. By doing so, we can expand our horizons, gain new perspectives, and deepen our connection with our partners.

In addition to personal growth, growth and self-discovery in relationships also involves examining our beliefs and behaviors in the context of our relationships. This can include exploring issues related to communication, conflict resolution, and intimacy. By doing so, we can gain a deeper understanding of our own motivations and behaviors, as well as our partner's, and work towards improving our relationships.

One important aspect of growth and self-discovery in relationships is the idea of mutual growth. This means that both partners are willing to grow and change, not only for themselves but for the benefit of the relationship as a whole. By embracing mutual growth, couples can build a stronger and more resilient relationship, and be better equipped to navigate the challenges that arise over time.

In conclusion, growth and self-discovery play a critical role in the success of relationships. By embracing vulnerability, exploring new interests and perspectives, and examining our own beliefs and behaviors, we can build strong and healthy relationships based on love, intimacy, and mutual growth.

Moving forward with confidence and hope.

After working through our emotional baggage, embracing vulnerability, and opening up to love, it is important to move forward with confidence and hope. This means having a positive outlook on the future of our relationships and believing in the possibility of true love and connection.

One of the key ways to move forward with confidence and hope is to let go of the past. This means letting go of past hurts, old grudges, and negative patterns that have held us back in previous relationships. By doing so, we free ourselves to build healthier and more fulfilling relationships in the future.

Another important factor in moving forward with confidence and hope is building self-awareness and self-confidence. This means understanding our own needs, values, and boundaries, and being confident in communicating them to our partners. It also means being confident in our own worth and ability to attract healthy and loving relationships.

In order to build self-awareness and self-confidence, it is important to engage in self-reflection and personal growth. This can include therapy, journaling, and other forms of self-expression. By exploring our own thoughts and feelings, we gain a deeper understanding of ourselves and what we truly want and need in a relationship.

It is also important to cultivate a support network of friends and family who believe in us and support us in our relationships. Having a supportive network can provide us with the encouragement and support we need to move forward with confidence and hope, even in the face of challenges.

Finally, it is important to have a positive and optimistic outlook on the future of our relationships. This means focusing on the potential for growth and connection, rather than dwelling on past hurts or setbacks. By doing so, we open ourselves up to the possibility of building strong, loving relationships that bring us happiness and fulfillment.

"In the end, love is a journey, and the more we embrace vulnerability, open our hearts, and move forward with confidence and hope, the closer we come to finding the fulfilling relationships we deserve. So let's take a deep breath, trust in the journey, and step forward into the unknown with open arms, ready to embrace the possibilities of love..."